REACH THE
SWEETNESS
OF PRAYER

Reach the Sweetness of Prayer

First published in Malaysia by
Tertib Publishing
23-2 Jalan PJS 5/30
Petaling Jaya Commercial City (PJCC)
46150 Petaling Jaya, Selangor
Malaysia

Tel: +603 7772 3156

First Edition: August 2019
Second Edition: February 2020

Cataloguing in-Publication Data is available from the National
Library of Malaysia

ISBN: 978-967-17402-2-4

Cover design: Zahin Zulkipli
Transcription: Faslin Syarina Salim
Typesetting & Layout: Ainul Syuhada
Printed by: Firdaus Press Sdn. Bhd.

Contents

Preface

In the name of Allah the Beneficent, the Most Merciful.

The Prayer is the most special connection between a person and his/her Lord. It sets the tone for everything in a Muslim's life. It is easy to slip into a rhythm of prayer that is dead an empty. This will only lead to a sick heart. Prayer originates deep in the heart and unfolds organically into words and body movements that beautifully give voice and shape to that deep love of the Divine echoing in the heart.

In this book you will find advice that will help you pray in a state of presence and connection. A way that will help you rhyme with the universal symphony of devotion and connection to the Almighty that everything in the universe sings in unison. The content of this book is based on talks and lectures that I shared online over many years of my own quest to find meaning and depth in my Prayer. We left the words of these talks mainly as they are without much editing to maintain the spontaneous nature of the delivery. Thus as you read, try to imagine you are listening to these words in their conversational, unrehearsed, crude format of delivery.

It is my hope that the content of this book and the experience it offers you will be a means to blow the soul back in your prayer and help you experience the prayer at a more profound level of presence and connection.

It takes sincerity and hard work to act on the suggestion found in this book. It takes patience and perseverance to see results. And most importantly, it takes complete trust in Allah and an honest sense of surrender that He is the only One who can give you khushu' in your Salah. When you let Him lead the way in the Prayer and stop overdoing focus and humility, you are more likely to feel khushu' naturally emerging in your experience.

Wish you all the best on this journey.

Moutasem al-Hameedy

REACH THE
SWEETNESS
OF PRAYER

There is a strong connection between the manner in which a person prays and what his position will be in Paradise. There is a strong connection between your rank in Paradise and the amount of khushu' – focus – that you find in your prayer. These are not my words, but I will mention who's in the later part, Insha Allah.

Imagine a man with a beard walks in the masjid, then he prays and in the middle of the prayer, he plays with his beard. Do you think this person is concentrating on what he is doing in his prayer?

Where does focus or concentration or khushu' take place? It is in the heart. Yet, you cannot see this man's heart. His focus is in the heart, but you made a judgement about his heart without being able to see his heart. You saw his external behaviour and you pass a judgement on his heart. Why?

There is a very strong connection between your heart and your actions. It is impossible for someone to be interested in something, yet not have his actions gravitating towards that thing which he loves. Wherever the heart goes, the actions will flow.

If you have noticed, I have been paraphrasing a statement from the Prophet s.a.w. In a sahih hadith recorded by Imam Al-Bukhari, the Messenger of Allah s.a.w said, "... There is a piece of flesh in the body if it becomes good (reformed) the whole body becomes good but if it gets spoilt the whole body gets spoilt and that is the heart." Therefore, the secret of a human being is the heart.

Obviously, your judgement cannot be final. This is why we are not supposed to judge people's intentions. But roughly speaking, it is a strong clue that when you see someone's external behaviour, you will have a good idea of what is going on in the heart.

When you see someone is playing around with their beard or probably looking at their watch or maybe even searching their pockets, you would automatically think this man does not have khushu' in his prayer and he is not really concentrating. That is a valid statement because that is exactly what the Prophet s.a.w said. At the time of the Prophet s.a.w, there was a man praying by himself in the masjid and he was playing around with his beard. The Prophet s.a.w made a beautiful statement as the companions were watching this man, "Had the heart of this man been in a state of khushu', it would have reflected on his limbs."

Iman is in the heart?

Someone who commits haram actions, they do not pray, they might drink, they might do different sorts of bad things, and when you give them advice, they say, "Iman is in the heart". We know that this guy does not know what he is talking about. It does not make sense because what is in the heart is reflected in the actions.

Therefore, if your actions are evil, be sure that there is something wrong with your heart. If your heart is in good shape, definitely it is going to reflect in your actions. As simple as that.

The challenge

Our challenge is to find out the sweetness in salah. Do you feel the sweetness as you perform your salah every day? Do you experience that kind of khushu' and that peaceful state of mind every day in your salah? Or do you experience this feeling at least once a week? Or perhaps once a month or once a year?

We have two extremes here: You do not experience that at all or you experience that at least once a week. There is a very interesting phenomenon that we will see later.

The Prophet's style of teaching

The style of teaching that we use with our kids and probably our friends (and even ourselves sometimes) is to go and learn some principles and start teaching people how they should behave. We always tell the kids "Okay in the presence of elderly people, do not talk, remain silent", or "When we go to the shop, do not trouble me", or "When you go to the school, do this. When you come to the masjid, do that." And so on and so forth. Most of the time, the kids do not abide by this. Because we are not using the Prophet's style of teaching.

One day, something happened in Madinah, in the house of one of the Ansar. Abdurrahman ibn 'Auf was there, Hamzah ibn Abdul Mutalib was there, and some other companions were there, too.

Ali ibn Abi Talib wanted to marry Fatimah, the daughter of Prophet Muhammad s.a.w, but he sat at home, feeling frustrated about something. He had a maid, an elderly woman. The maid approached Ali r.a and said, "Somebody asked for the hand of Fatimah. Are you going to stay at home forever? When are you going to take action?"

Guess who asked for the hand of Fatimah? Abu Bakar As-Siddiq r.a asked for Fatimah's hand in marriage. But the Prophet s.a.w did not accept his proposal. Umar r.a approached the Prophet s.a.w and it was not accepted too. Then, Ali's maid approached him and said, "Go and do something." Ali r.a said, "What can I do? I do not have anything I can offer her as a mahr." The woman replied, "Well, just go to the Prophet s.a.w and we will find a way." So he went to see the Prophet s.a.w and he sat there. Zayd ibn Harithah r.a was with the Prophet s.a.w.

Ali ibn Abi Talib r.a sat there feeling shy. He did not know how to initiate a proposal. The Prophet s.a.w looked at him and said, "O Ali, why did you come here?" Ali r.a replied "Nothing." The Prophet s.a.w said, "Maybe you come here to ask for the hand of Fatimah?" In a very fatherly fashion. Ali r.a was baffled by the question.

The Prophet s.a.w then asked, "Why are you hesitant?" Ali r.a replied, "I have nothing to offer her." The Prophet s.a.w said, "What happened to the armour that I gave you in the time of Badr?" Ali ibn Abi Talib r.a replied, "It is worth nothing."

Previously, Ali r.a had two camels. Camels were very expensive at that time. If you had a camel, you were considered to be relatively rich. Ali r.a lost his two camels in one day. It had to do with Hamzah r.a and Abdurrahman ibn 'Auf r.a.

Before Ali r.a wanted to approach Fatimah r.ha, he got himself ready with the two camels. One of the camels he got from the spoils of the war of Badr and another one was given to him by the Prophet s.a.w. Ali r.a was trying to get cash in order to marry Fatimah. So, he left the camels in the market and he went to deal with some business with a man. When he came back, both of his camels were cut into pieces. Ali r.a could not believe when he saw it. Camels were gone, his dreams vanished. He was about 23 years old at that time. Ali r.a then cried.

When Ali r.a rushed into the Prophet's place in tears, the Prophet s.a.w asked, "What's wrong? What happened?" Ali r.a said, "Hamzah slaughtered my camels." And he did not do anything with them, did not eat them or prepare them for food; he just cut the camels into pieces and throw them.

The Prophet s.a.w wanted to find out more of the story, so he went to the Ansari's house. When he walked into the house and saw Hamzah, he asked, "Why did you do that?" Hamzah r.a looked at the Prophet s.a.w from head to toe and then he looked at Ali r.a and said, "You are only slaves that belong to my father." That was Hamzah. Do you know why? He was drunk. That was before khamr was made haram.

The point behind this story is that most of the time, the Prophet s.a.w did not give his companions direct instructions. Most of his teachings were not direct instructions. The Prophet s.a.w would give the general frame for people; belief in Allah, explain to them the meaning of life, put them in the right mindset, and then everything would go in the right direction. That is the reason most of our teachings are not effective. Because we try to tell people what to do, but we never put them in the right mindset.

The Prophet s.a.w would always make use of whatever situation he was in to teach people. That is the best way you teach people.

There was someone who managed to get his young age children to prefer death than drugs. They would never come close to touch drugs or people who use drugs. How did he do it? From an early age, this man took his children to a multi-storey car park that was full of drug addicts and it was saturated with the smell of urine and all these filth. When the children saw people in that state, they associated a lot of disgust and hatred for drugs. Late after that, his kids were exposed to drugs so many times but drugs were always out of the question to them.

That is exactly how we should teach our children. Give them a real-life experience rather than just keep telling them how things should be. Therefore, the Prophet s.a.w was actually teaching the companions something when he said, "Had the heart of this man been in a state of khushu', it would have reflected on his limbs" when they saw a man playing with his beard while praying in the mosque. Whenever you see something, teach your children or your friends. Seize the opportunity to teach them something real. It sinks in a hundred times better than bringing a hundred books and tell your kids, "Learn this. Learn that." The experience incorporates more senses.

"Pray as you have seen me pray"

If we want to find the sweetness in the prayer, our focus should not be primarily on the physical reality of the prayer. The Prophet s.a.w said, "Pray as you have seen me pray." Why is this? Because that is how we should pray. If we pray in the manner in which the Prophet s.a.w prayed, we will find a huge difference in our salah. And this is the factor number one in having the sweetness in salah.

Where do we get this from? We get this from the fact that Allah is The All Wise (Al Hakeem). What does wise means? In Arabic, al-hakeem means the one who does not do things for no reason. Everything in Islam is carefully chosen by Allah s.w.t. The smallest thing in Islam that you might think is trivial, unimportant, insignificant has a reason that Allah s.w.t made it that way. And it has an impact that you should expect from it.

Often people would say, "It does not make any difference that you put your hand here or here, or whether you take your hands up when you say Allahu akbar, or whether you put your hands on your knees when you make ruku'. What difference does it make? I am just making a salah." Yes, ultimately you are making a salah, but everything that the Prophet s.a.w did in his prayer is significance.

Allah s.w.t says in surah Al-A'raf, "To Allah belong the creation and to Allah belong the legislation." Two things – creation and legislation. Allah s.w.t created us in a certain format. Physically, emotionally, mentally, psychologically, even socially, and he sent down the way of life that is completely compatible with our creation. Just like a lock and its key. You cannot open that lock except with its key. That is exactly how Islam works with our human nature.

When Allah s.w.t describes the Prophet s.a.w, He said, "If he were to follow your desires and your preferences, you would put yourselves in extreme hardships." Subhanallah. Even in your seeking ease, you will ultimately put yourself in hardship.

The economic crisis in the world is a clear example. People want ease and deficiency of control in terms of their financial system. This is why riba or interest is halal for them. A lot of the manipulation that is taking place in the financial and economic worlds only cause hardship in people's lives.

That is exactly what the above verse is saying. Allah s.w.t sent Islam in all its details compatible with our nature. If we missed out on any point, there is going to be a difference. Even where you place your hands in salah does make a difference. Allah s.w.t does not legislate anything except for a reason. Therefore, the way the Prophet s.a.w prayed is one excellent way to help you reach your khushu'. But that could take you probably halfway through.

Definition of khushu'

What could bring about the sweetness of prayer? If you understand the concept of khushu'. How do you define khushu'? You might say humility. Meanwhile, concentration is not exactly khushu' although it leads to that state. Sincerity is also not the definition of khushu' itself, but it is strongly related.

Khushu' is when the heart is connected to Allah s.w.t in a prayer. This is the secret of salah. Allah s.w.t says in surah Ar-Ra'd, "Those who have believed and the hearts find comfort, tranquillity in the mention (or the remembrance) of Allah; indeed, with the remembrance of Allah, the hearts are at ease (and in the state of tranquillity)."

Do you know who experiences khushu' the most these days? Including outside of salah? Lovers. What is the essence of khushu'? Connection to Allah. What do lovers have? Connection to their beloved ones. What happened?

They develop this focus for the person they love. Have you ever seen someone who is truly in love? Could you ever have a proper conversation with that person? Impossible. Because whatever you talk about, they are going to always gravitate to the person they love. What is this? This is khushu' – devotion and connection. This is what we need to have with Allah s.w.t (and even better than that). That is Ibn al-Qayyim's analogy.

How to develop khushu'?

Firstly, be in love with Allah s.w.t. Take this as a general rule and perhaps have it written and hang it on the wall.

Whatever you love and attach to, will be on your mind in prayers. Try it out. Recall what was on your mind during your recent salah. If it is not Allah s.w.t, then you need to recheck your heart.

How do we love Allah? It is by knowing Him. However, you might think you know Allah s.w.t, but is this the case?

When you love someone, you become motivated to learn more about them. The more you learn about them, the more you love them. The more you love them, the more you are curious to know more about them. It is an upward spiral. This is exactly the case with Allah s.w.t.

How do we think we can know Allah? The most common way for many people is to learn the 99 names of Allah. This is a good idea, but how much did you learn especially the meanings and the implications? This should not be just a classroom lesson. We need to learn these names in real-life situations. For example, someone is in trouble. You start to help them, go through their problem, and link everything you do towards the names and attributes of Allah s.w.t. Only then your heart will start to be connected to Allah.

Reading through the Quran is a good experience. However, most of us do not do enough contemplation and this is why we do not get enough. In terms of reading through the word, a lot of us do not do it the right way. Instead of tracing everything back to Allah s.w.t, we get taken by the beauty of His creation and we stop halfway.

So how do we get to know Allah s.w.t? There is no one specific way. We need to do all of these together. Also, think about this question: How often do you read the letters of Allah s.w.t? Do you feel an attachment as you read the Quran?

There was an old woman who cannot read and write. She had a son who studies in a different country. In the first month of her son abroad, he sent her a letter. The woman brought the letter to her neighbour to get the lady's help in reading it. The second month when the letter arrived, she got her neighbour to help her read again. In the third month, the neighbour went on a holiday. The old woman had to wait for her other son to come back from school to help her read the letter. Then she finally taught herself how to read and write. She literally learned how to read and write just to read her son's letters. This shows how much she loves her son.

So how much do you love Allah s.w.t? Keep the answer to yourself based on how often you read the Quran.

Shaykh Abdurrahman As-Sa'di said in one of his books, "For people who think khushu' is a matter of salah, they do not understand what khushu' is. Khushu' is a continuous state of mind. If you want khushu' in salah, you need to have it outside salah."

In another beautiful statement, Shaykh Saleh Al-Maghamsi said, "Salah is a privilege. In salah, you are standing before Allah s.w.t. and that is privilege and honour that Allah does not give to anyone. On top of this, khushu' is the pinnacle. Therefore, Allah will not give it to someone who contradicts the meaning of salah in his life." So he said that if you want khushu', you need to have khushu' in your transactions. Khushu' in the way you treat your brothers, sisters, parents, and even everyone. You need khushu' in doing your job.

It is all connected. You will never have khushu' in salah unless you have it in all aspects of your life. Human beings have consistency in our fitrah. Allah s.w.t says that He did not put two hearts to anyone in his chest. You do not have two hearts. You cannot have two different orientations. You might have an inner conflict for a while, but ultimately you will reach one.

Mu'adh ibn Jabal r.a said, "Hearts have different types. One that is completely saturated with good orientations and that is the heart that has light in it. Then, there is a heart that is completely saturated with evil orientations. And lastly, there is a heart situated in the middle; sometimes it is here, sometimes it is there. A heart that has two elements; iman and kufr. Ultimately, one of them is going to take over."

Therefore, you cannot be connected to Allah s.w.t in the mosque and disconnected outside. Khushu' is the connection that you have in salah and outside salah. If you want to have khushu', you need to change your life. You need to align your life behind salah. If you do not align your life behind the love of Allah s.w.t and salah, you can never have khushu'.

Learning the Quran

Another way to know more about Allah s.w.t, to love Him, and eventually to reach khushu' is to read the Quran and reflects upon it. Learning the surahs without understanding the real meanings is not a good thing. Learn one surah, learn the meaning, and try to implement them. See how they relate to who you are. Take it seriously.

It is important to know that learning is not storing information. Learning is being. If you do not absorb what you learn and it does not become part of who you are, if it does not mix with your blood and your flesh, and it does not change you, then you have wasted your time. If you think learning is just a mental process, you are not going to benefit anything from it.

Allah is Ar-Rahman and Ar-Rahim

This is not a simple thing to learn. You need to see this in everything you go through, even when you get in trouble. If you have truly learned the meaning of Ar-Rahman and Ar-Rahim, you would see the mercy of Allah s.w.t in a trial. You would be able to see through.

When Ibn Taymiyyah (may Allah has mercy on him) was in Damascus, the Khalifah of the Muslim who was in Egypt at that time sent a troop to arrest him. They handcuffed Ibn Taymiyyah and dragged him while riding their horses. Ibn Taymiyyah was on foot from Damascus to Cairo, which would take about 20 days to a month.

As Ibn Taymiyyah was dragged out of his city, his

students said, "O Imam, this is the time for patience." He looked at them and said, "No, this is the time for thankfulness." He was on a different level. He said, "By God, there is a sense of contentment in my heart that if it were to be distributed among the people of Damascus, it would be enough for each one of them."

It is because Ibn Taymiyyah could see through that plight. He is the man who really understood the meaning of the names and attributes of Allah s.w.t.

Where you are in Paradise

The manner in which you pray in your prayer reflects where you are in Paradise (or where you are at the sight of Allah s.w.t). This is a statement by Imam Ahmad ibn Hanbal.

A lot of people say that they wish they can know where they will be in Paradise. We all have high hopes about that. Therefore we refer to the above statement by Imam Ahmad. Just look at our salah.

You are thinking about the next business project you have, or your next journey, or the woman you love, or the money you lost last week, or the next football game, or any usual concerns; in the prayer and you say, "I will be very close to the Prophet s.a.w in Paradise". You will be fooling yourself. Your concentration in prayers reflects where you are. Therefore, take it seriously.

Do not procrastinate either because life never gives you the opportunity to focus in your prayers. Shaytan has dedicated his life just for your prayers. There is a shaytan which his full-time job is to distract you in the prayer. His name is Khinzab (or Khinzib). That is your enemy. This is why in the prayer, as soon as you say "Allahu akbar", you have engaged in a battle against the shaytan. He is jumping up and down, approaching your left and right, reminding you of everything. We need to be more enthusiastic about our salah just as Khinzab is enthusiastic about distracting us.

Qiblah

According to some classification, we all have physical reality and spiritual reality (soul). The heart is connected to the soul mainly. Your heart impacts your body and your body impacts your heart.

The direction of qiblah was not chosen just like that. Obviously, in science, they could find some secrets in this. But, there is something about human behaviour – if you feel good, there are physical signs. And if you feel down, there are other physical signs.

If you feel energetic, you will find your shoulders up. You do not do that deliberately, it just happens. And if you feel down, you will find your shoulders down too. Let's imagine a moment where everything was going perfect and life was so rosy, more than you wanted to be. You felt so happy about it. Then think about the most miserable moment in your life when you felt down, nothing was working out and all seem to be hopeless. Go back to that thoughts and re-live it. If you focus enough, you can feel the patterns.

When Allah s.w.t makes us perform the prayer in a certain way, it has an impact on our heart. Therefore when we face the qiblah, there is a sense of unity that brings the Muslims together. Something more important is the fact that we physically face the qiblah – it is some kind of direction in our heart when facing Allah s.w.t. In other words, while our body faces the qiblah, our heart faces Allah s.w.t.

A khushu' man and a lion

Imam Adh-Dhahabi shares a story in his book. There was a group of people traveling at night and they stopped at a valley. As they were getting themselves ready to sleep, a lion came about. They jumped up the trees, taking shelter. But there was one person who has already started his qiyamullail. He was praying his night prayer. The lion came and this man did not move. He kept praying. The lion walked around the man and then it left. When the other men came down from the trees, they said, "The lion was here and you did not move." The man said, "By God, I felt shy that I am standing before Allah s.w.t and I fear one of His creation." What level of khushu' is that?

The big secret

The secret is mentioned in the Quran but indirectly. Allah s.w.t says, "The believers are successful; they are the ones who are khushu' in their prayer." Some of the scholars of tafseer said that this is the first description of the believers. Therefore, if you want to know if a person has iman or not, look at his prayer. And here we learn that the reason for khushu' is iman.

Read again the same verse mentioned above. In Arabic, the sequence of the descriptions has logic to it. So why did Allah say these believers are successful and they are the ones who have khushu' in salah? The scholars of tafseer said that it means iman is the essence and that is the signs of iman; they have khushu' in salah. The more iman you have, the more khushu' you are going to have.

The second indirect sign in the Quran is the verse, "And seek help in the patience and the prayer; indeed the prayer is difficult except for the ones who are khushu'"

Then Allah s.w.t describes the ones who are khushu' – they have faith and conviction that they will return to Allah.

If you truly believe that you will meet Allah s.w.t on the Day of Judgement and that is your ultimate destiny, you will gain khushu' in your salah. So the more you believe, the more khushu' you will have.

The next secret is also from the Quran. But the one who uses it best is shaytan. Shaytan knows human nature and how to manipulate it. There are two things that control everything we do. Shaytan uses them to get Adam a.s and Eve to eat from the tree.

Imagine, Allah s.w.t put Adam and Eve in Paradise – they get everything they want, they can do what they want, take what they want, wish for what they want and they will get it, but they must never come near that one tree.

Despite their belief in Allah, their devotion, and their knowledge about Allah s.w.t, shaytan managed to get Adam and Eve to eat from that tree. Shaytan pulled two strings, which are mentioned in surah Al-A'la.

Allah s.w.t reprimands humanity when he says, "You prefer this worldly life. And the akhirah is better and more everlasting." These are the two things that control our behaviour.

What did shaytan say to Adam a.s in order to get him to eat from that tree? He said, "Shall I not show you the tree that will grant you eternal life and kingship (or you get everything you want)?" And Adam ate from the tree.

So that is what affects our behaviour – the time horizon of something and its level of goodness. We always aim for the best and what lasts longer. If you link these two things to salah, you will have complete focus. That is what Imam Al-Ghazali says in Ihya' Ulumuddin. He said, "If you truly get yourself to believe that Allah is better for you and your relationship with Allah is more everlasting, and you know the prayer is the vehicle to that, you could never think of anything else during your salah."

If someone tells you, "I will give you a job and you will get $1,000 a month and it is for three years. And I will give you another job for twenty years and you will get $5,000 a month. Which one would you choose?" Apparently, we would choose the second job.

When a person falls into zina, they go through a state of mind. They think that desire is tacit, but they cannot think of anything other than this feeling or this enjoyment that they are going to have. That moment seems everlasting. The same with riba and any sins. Shaytan will always give you the impression that this thing is everlasting.

Subhanallah, this is, in fact, a psychological phenomenon. They called it Learned Optimism. The opposite of it is Learned Helplessness.

Some people who always fail to do things, they think that is the story of their lives, they will be failures forever. This is learned helplessness. Shaytan always plays with our time horizon. So when you are about to fall into sins, he just puts you under the impression that you do not see beyond it, that it seems like your whole life is there. You will feel like it is something you can never live without. But you do not realize it.

Therefore remember, whatever you do, do it because deep down in your heart you believe it is better and it is more lasting. Try to link that to your prayers. Compare the salah to your business meeting. How long is it going to last? Two years later, you will not even think about that business meeting. But what about the salah? It is more everlasting, it is our connection to Allah s.w.t. It has to do with the hereafter. If you use this kind of logic, you will be surprised at how much focus will start to gravitate to your salah. The real business deal with Allah is the salah.

Conclusion

Remember that khushu' is not restricted to the prayer. It is a way of life, a state of mind, and it is a continuous stream. If we do not keep up with it throughout our different activities in life, we will not be able to command it at the time we stand before Allah s.w.t.

TIPS TO
MASTER KHUSHU'

Introduction

How beautiful it is to be in nature, in the natural creation of Allah s.w.t. We feel the serenity, the peace, and the tranquility because this whole creation engages and celebrating the glory of Allah s.w.t.

Allah s.w.t says, "There is nothing except that it celebrates the glory of Allah s.w.t and it praises Allah s.w.t." This is where you get all these peace.

But you know, Allah s.w.t has given us a more profound gift which gives us more serenity, more peace, and more tranquility. We can access that in our salah or prayer. It is the state of khushu'. Khushu' is a spiritual state where you sort of engage with the core of your humanity. It has to do with your fitrah, the natural dispositions that we are worshippers of Allah, we are people who love Allah, we are people who fear Allah, and we are people who seek Allah s.w.t. It is such a deep state.

We can access khushu' in our salah, but we have to do our salah well. There are secrets to how to access this beautiful state of khushu'. It is when you experience the sweetness of iman and faith. There are ways to do that. Insha Allah I will be sharing with you tips where we can master khushu'. If you take these advice and act on them consistently and put your heart and soul in them, you could truly transform your khushu'.

I hope you find these tips powerful and beneficial. This is our gift to you but it places responsibility and expectation on you – to take it seriously, take it to heart, engage in it, practice it, experiment with it, and try your best to get everything from these tips. I promise that the more you invest in Allah s.w.t, He will give you always more and the fruit will be greater, will be more beneficial, will be beyond your expectations.

There is no state in this world that is more beautiful than being connected to Allah, engaging with Allah s.w.t in the state of khushu'.

#1 Gratitude

Pray your prayer in a state of gratitude

I believe this is extremely powerful. See yourself in the receiving end. Do not see yourself doing Allah favour as you perform salah, but see yourself as receiving that favour from Allah s.w.t. He taught you how to pray, He inspired you to pray, He allowed you to pray, He observes you as you pray, He accepts prayer from you, He allows you to pray consistently, He rewards you for your prayer. It is all about you receiving from Allah s.w.t.

Had it not been for Allah s.w.t who has written that you pray, you would not pray at all. So, this is a gift from Allah s.w.t. This will inspire you and put you in a state of gratitude – thankfulness. You would see yourself receiving such a powerful and great gift from Allah s.w.t when you allow yourself to settle in this state of gratitude. And as you engage your salah in this beautiful state, you will find a lot of khushu' that you have been looking for.

Do that everyday, put your heart in it and insha Allah it will help you.

#2 Sincerity

Pray your salah in a state of sincerity

As simple as it may seem to say such, do your salah for Allah s.w.t. Although this seems to be obvious, but most of the time we are not doing it right.

You need to think of Allah s.w.t. You need to consider your relationship with Allah s.w.t. You need to feel that you owe Allah s.w.t so much and that He deserves your full attention and He deserves your best.

Before you begin your salah, get in that state of wanting to give Allah s.w.t something special – that this salah is only about Him and you. It is just between you and Him. That's it. So when you do your salah, perform it as an expression of your love to Allah s.w.t. Express your love as you are performing your salah. Make everything in it as manifestation of the love you have for Allah in your heart – in your recitation, in your adhkar, in your body movement – and see the magic happens in your salah.

#3 Pray as the Prophet Prayed

Learn how the Prophet s.a.w performed his salah

In order to get a great deal of khushu' and the state of engagement and immersion in your salah, you need to pay attention to the details of your salah.

Check a video that authentically describes how the Prophet s.a.w prayed. Or read one of those books that describes how the Prophet s.a.w prayed. Learn how to pray as the Prophet s.a.w prayed. This is the physical vessel for your salah. When you do it right and then you tune in to your heart to connect to Allah s.w.t, this vessel will protect your salah and will help it reach heights you never imagine. The physical vessel – the physical frame – of your salah is extremely powerful.

However, do not dwell so much on the physicality. After you learn it, it becomes automatic. Just focus on the beautiful connection between you and Allah s.w.t.

#4 Mindset

Put your heart and soul in your prayer

Basically when you pray your salah, make sure you get yourself in a mindset of doing your best. I would say: Put your heart and soul in your prayer. It seems obvious, but we do not do it.

When I say "Put your heart" it means put everything you have, put your all in the process of prayer. It is only about 10 minutes. Just put everything you have; energy and attention in this beautiful moment and standing in the presence of Allah s.w.t and leave the world behind.

Make it a challenge to get every salah to be the best ever in your life. Raise the bar with every salah and let your heart go deep right into this ibadah. Do it with full attention and intention. Let your soul fly you right into the salah and you will see that you can actually connect to Allah s.w.t in ways you never imagine.

#5 Your Best is Not Enough

You can never give Allah what He truly deserves

When you engage in your salah, remind yourself of one important thing: No matter what you do, you can never pay Allah s.w.t back. You can never give Allah s.w.t what He truly deserves. In a sense, even your best is not enough.

However, this should not be a reason for despair. This should actually be a very effective motivator. Realizing the greatness of The One you stand before. Realizing that no matter what you do, Allah s.w.t is far greater, deserves much more. And this could actually compel you to always do more for the sake of Allah, to try to step up your game, try to give Allah s.w.t a better salah every time you stand in His presence. Basically it makes the salah a very challenging and it gives a sense of competition.

Even though what you do is not enough, Allah s.w.t accepts from you. He appreciates it, He rewards it for you, and He helps you do more of it. This is such a beautiful state to be in.

#6 Ihsan

When you worship Allah, do it as if you are seeing Him

There is something extremely helpful you can do in your salah. This is what we know in Islam as Ihsan.

Ihsan is basically to do everything to a point of perfection. It is that when you pray your salah, at that moment you offer Allah s.w.t your best. When you are doing it, you are aware that you are in the presence of Allah s.w.t. In a hadith recorded by Imam Muslim, the Prophet s.a.w describes Ihsan as you worship Allah as if you are seeing Him.

If you fail to reach that point, there is a second level. It is to worship Allah s.w.t in a state where you just being aware that He observes you all the time. This should not be as a source to put you off or something that strikes only fear in your heart. But it should strike hope in your heart that Allah s.w.t is observing you and you want to offer something to Allah that would please Him. So when you offer something really great, you actually want to reach your perfection or ihsan.

#7 Perfect Timings

Reflect on the wisdom of the time of salah

We often jump right into the prayer where we pray mindlessly – without our mind and our heart being in it.

There is one thing that will help put you in that right mood to perform your salah in a beautiful way. It is to reflect on the wisdom of the time of your salah.

Salah are not designed or assigned randomly or haphazardly. Allah s.w.t has a point behind everything. In Fajr, you start your day with Allah s.w.t – with a powerful state of connection; spirituality and gratitude to Allah s.w.t. Then, during the day you have Dhuhr and Asr. If you get swept off your feet into this world, you will lose connection with Allah s.w.t and you will lose sight of your ultimate goal with Him. Thereafter you close your day with Maghrib prayer where you sort of submit that day and hand it over to Allah s.w.t, thank Him for that, and appreciate what He has given and allows you to do. Before you go to sleep, you pray Isha and that is basically to seal your day completely and continue in a state of connection with Allah s.w.t.

You start you day and you finish you day with Allah s.w.t. When you reflect on this, you will have full appreciation to Allah s.w.t.

#8 Spiritual Cleansing

The sins that you have committed will be wiped away with wudu

When you make wudu for your salah or when you rinse parts of your body, there is wisdom behind it. The Prophet s.a.w told us in one hadith that when you engage in wudu, basically the sins that you have committed with your hands, your eyes, your mouth, will be wiped with the water as you are rinsing your organs. (Recorded by Imam Muslim) This is a real spiritual experience.

You need to see yourself being cleansed of all the sins as you are making wudu. This will heighten your attention and will get you in the state of a proper khushu' before you even engage in your salah. You will feel that you are approaching salah having cleansed part of – or maybe all of – your sins if you have done your wudu properly.

The next time you make wudu, just be mindful of the sins being washed away and feel the blessings of Allah s.w.t in this beautiful process.

#9 Garment of Taqwa

Covering awrah leads to inner or spiritual beautification

Before you engage in your salah, you obviously have to dress up properly. You have to cover your awrah and be in a presentable shape because you are standing in the presence of Allah s.w.t. This is not random. Focus on the fact that Allah s.w.t does not command us with anything randomly. There is a great lesson behind it.

When you cover your awrah, you basically presenting yourself to Allah s.w.t in the best shape. You are engaging in a form of physical beautification. This is actually leading to a process of inner or spiritual beautification, because it covers your sins and shortcomings.

#10 A Standing of Honor

Imagine you are standing in the presence of Allah s.w.t

Before you say "Allahu Akbar", focus on one thing that will help you immensely: Remind yourself of the context you are standing in. You are standing before Allah s.w.t – The Creator of the heavens and the earth.

The Prophet s.a.w said in a hadith, "When one of you stands in a prayer, Allah erects His face in front of His servant (in a way that befits Allah's majesty)." That means you are standing in the presence of Allah, The King of Kings! Do you realize this?

Tune into this context. I am now standing in the presence of Allah s.w.t for this much of time. When you stand in front of someone important – someone you love or appreciate – you feel grateful and favoured. Imagine you are standing in the presence of Allah s.w.t. Make sure throughout your salah you are aware of this.

#11 The Secrets of the Call for Prayer

Focus on the adhan and take advantage of it

We usually think we can find khushu' if we just engage in our salah; start reciting, doing the adhkar, then ruku', sujood, and so on and so forth. However, we missed out on an important thing that gives us a head start. For example, adhan – the call for prayer. It is not random. There is a reason why there is a call for prayer with every salah. There is a reason why the call for prayer has certain wording and meaning. These meaning and words awaken something in your heart that really helps you tune into the state of khushu' even before you start your salah.

Therefore, next time when it is time for salah, listen to the adhan. You might say, "I live in a non-Muslim country, we do not have adhan because the masajid do not make adhan loudly". Well you have it on your phone, on your laptop, or any device. Get the app and when adhan calls out, listen to it completely and focus on the meaning.

Allah is Greater

I bear witness that there is no god except Allah

I bear witness that Muhammad is the messenger of Allah

Hurry to the prayer

Hurry to success

Allah is Greater

There is no god except Allah

When you contemplate on all these meanings, they will give you head start into the khushu' process in your salah.

#12 The Secrets of Turning to Qiblah

Qiblah is the first house ever built for the worship of Allah s.w.t on this earth

There is something that extremely important but very easy and it helps you get more khushu' in your salah. As you are standing to start your prayer, you face the qiblah. This is a very dynamic act. This is a huge engagement because the qiblah is the first house ever built for the worship of Allah s.w.t on this earth.

The qiblah is like a magnet for the souls. This is why when you face the qiblah, it is not only a physical act. When your face turn towards the qiblah, your heart turns to Allah s.w.t at the same time. As you are facing the qiblah, you are doing the same act to the same direction. All of the prophets and messengers of Allah, the companions, and Muslims around the globe face the same spot. That spot connected to the heaven where the angels worship in Bait Al-Ma'mur.

#13 When Hearts Unite

As you are praying, feel the unity among the Muslims.

Before you start your salah, you obviously have to face the qiblah. Facing the qiblah is such a powerful exercise and it connects you to Allah s.w.t because there is something special about the qiblah, which is the Kaabah.

In addition, let's focus on something that will help you (with the will of Allah) and enhance your khushu'. Remember that every Muslim throughout history, today, and in the future will be facing the same qiblah to worship Allah s.w.t. Therefore, the hearts are all geared and directed in that direction that gives you so much strength.

Facing the qiblah also gives us the importance of uniting the Muslims. Imagine the Muslims are praying in unison. As you are engaging in your salah, you find someone on the other side of the world who are facing this same qiblah. Your hearts somehow meet there. This should reminds you of the unity of the Muslims.

This belief in Allah s.w.t brings us together; not only in our heart but even in our physical direction. Feel the love that Allah s.w.t brought among those true believers and it will help you see that you are doing something great.

#14 Feel the Greatness of Allah

Focus on the meaning of "Allahu akbar" in your heart

As you have your intention to begin your salah, you then say "Allahu akbar". The word Allahu akbar should come first from your heart. You can do that. How?

Put your attention not only to the words, but also on your heart. Feel the meaning of the word Allahu akbar. You are glorifying Allah – there is nothing greater than Him, nothing more dominant than Him. Do not just focus on the word Allahu akbar, but focus also on the meaning that is in your heart. Your heart shall feel the glorious and the greatness of Allah s.w.t. When you do this, you feel the shivers run through your body.

The next time you say "Allahu akbar", immerse yourself completely into this word and focus on your heart so it feels the greatness of Allah s.w.t.

#15 Address Allah Directly

As you pray your salah, Allah is in front of you

This secret works with all aspects of the salah, all the times in salah. It is quite simple, but you just need to really pay attention to it and be sincere in performing it.

It suggests that as you are performing your salah, everything you say in the salah, you are saying it to Allah s.w.t. You are not alone as you pray your salah. Allah s.w.t is in front of you. You are standing in Allah's presence and you are addressing Him directly. Therefore, when you are making dua and reciting the Quran, you are speaking to Allah s.w.t and He is listening to you.

Put yourself in this mindset. Feeling that Allah s.w.t receives and listens to what you say should really get you more engage in what you are saying. It will be as though you mean what you say, since it comes from your heart.

#16 Active Reflection

What could possibly be the wisdom behind all acts in the prayer?

There is a beautiful principle that helps us increase the level of our khushu' in a progressive manner. Just focus on the fact that there is nothing random in the prayer. Everything is put in the right place, with the right manner, and at the right timing.

As you engage in your salah, reflect on everything and what it could possibly means to your relationship with Allah s.w.t. What could possibly be the wisdom behind it. Just raising your hand while saying "Allahu akbar" and showing your palm is such a powerful physical expression of surrender. You sort of surrendering to Allah s.w.t physically and your mental state is in agreement to this.

Therefore, do not undermine any parts of the salah. Everything in salah is purposeful and has its meaning, thus it will bring impact on you. When you engage in your salah and start searching for these meanings, then try to live them; you will get to raise the level of your khushu'.

#17 Starting on a Positive Note

Invest your focus in the Opening dua of the salah

When you start your salah, after saying "Allahu akbar", you are supposed to say the Opening dua (Iftitah). We have different versions of Opening dua from the Prophet s.a.w. Each one of them has a profound and beautiful meaning.

As you engage in the Opening dua, do not just say them. Do not just murmur the words – that is not the point. The point is that each dua gives rise to a different states and it serves as a warm-up for your engagement in your salah. It sorts of pushing you to a higher level of presence or connection to Allah s.w.t.

What you need to do to utilize this is to take the Opening dua seriously. Treat it as an extraordinary start for your salah. Engage in its meaning and see what it says – some of them glorify Allah s.w.t, some of them just indicate the nature of your relationship with Allah s.w.t, or some of them are about seeking forgiveness. Each one of them has such an intense impact in your heart and your state. And it gives you beautiful experience in your salah.

#18 Ask Allah for Protection

Say "A'udhubillahi min ash-shaytannirrajeem"

As you engage in your salah; you start with raising your hand while saying "Allahu akbar" and you recite the Opening dua. Then the Prophet s.a.w taught us something that is very important, which is mentioned by Allah s.w.t in the Quran – that when you recite the Quran, you seek refuge and protection in Allah from shaytan (the cursed one). Do not skip this. Do not rush to the prayer and skip this important thing.

These are not just words you simply say. This is a profound state that you are supposed to get yourself in. You are basically turning to Allah s.w.t in a state of helplessness, saying, "O Allah, I cannot help myself against shaytan. His influence is strong. He is after me. So, I need to turn to You to seek help from You, so I can deal with him and push him away from my salah."

When it comes to salah, shaytan will do his best to distract you so that you will not enjoy the state of khushu'. Therefore, when you seek protection in Allah s.w.t from shaytan, feel that you are helpless and that you trust in Allah.

#19 The Beauty of the Quran

Recite and reflect on the words of Allah

When you already started your salah with the Opening dua and you have seek protection in Allah s.w.t, now you are ready to start reciting the words of your Creator. Such a remarkable privilege!

There are billions of people who do not even know what the words of Allah are. But you are given the privilege to recite the words of Allah s.w.t. Therefore, appreciate that beautiful gift, see yourself in a bubble of care and blessings from Allah s.w.t – you are pampered by Allah s.w.t, you are favoured, you are given something that is extremely special. These are the words of your Creator and you are allowed to recite them and to reflect on them. It makes you want to be thankful to Allah s.w.t and give your full attention in your salah.

#20 The Power of Surah Al-Fatihah

Surah Al-Fatihah is an obligation in every prayer

When you engage in your salah, the first thing you read after the Opening dua is surah Al-Fatihah. Allah s.w.t makes this obligatory in every salah because the meanings of the verses in this surah are deep. They could shape your life if you pay attention to them and you recite from your heart.

In surah Al-Fatihah, you praise Allah s.w.t, then you reflect on the fact that He is The Most Merciful and Most Compassionate. You learn that Allah s.w.t is The Master of the Day of Judgement, only to Him we worship and only in Him that we seek help from. You then beg Allah s.w.t for His guidance, to make your life go right and to stay in the His path, and not to be one of those who cause His anger.

Live and reflect on surah Al-Fatihah as it will heighten your khushu' and strengthen your relationship with Allah s.w.t. Know that as you recite this surah, Allah s.w.t will respond to you as the Prophet s.a.w told us.

#21 Reflect on the Words of Allah

Invest on the reflection of the Quran that you recite

As you are engaged in your salah and you have already started with reciting surah Al-Fatihah, you are then going to recite something else. Whatever you recite, reflect on it. The words of the Quran are meaningful.

Allah s.w.t said that He sent down the Quran so that people may reflect and remember. Remember what? Basically awaken their fitrah – their natural state of loving Allah s.w.t, feeling Him, and wanting to worship Him.

The Quran is an open field of wisdom, knowledge, and impact that we should not dispense with. Therefore, when you are engaged in your salah, recite as much as possible of the Quran and do not just go through the verses. Make sure you are reflecting on what each verse is telling you, what is the message for you in this verse. These are the words of Allah, The Creator of the heavens and the earth. Each one of them has a lot of light and life in it. You surely want to get the light and you want to let that life revive you and revive your heart and your spirit.

#22 The Secrets of Ruku'

What is the purpose behind you going bow down to Allah s.w.t?

As you are engaged in your salah and you have already recited the Quran as you are standing, now it is time to go for ruku'. Such a significant experience. This experience is out of this world.

Somebody might ask the question, "Why don't we pray in this way? Why do we have to make some physical positions and stances, go for bowing and prostration? Why don't we just do like meditation? Like people sit still and they start going deep down or they calm down their thoughts or whatever in their contemplative state?"

Salah is different. There is purpose behind you going to bow down – put your head down before Allah s.w.t. There is a spiritual state you cannot access without putting your physical body in that position. There is a strong connection between your soul and your body. When your body is in that position, your soul tunes into a completely different state that is inaccessible to it otherwise. Therefore, engage in that beautiful state of ruku'. Allow yourself to devour it, enjoy it, and benefit from it.

#23 Complete Glorification

"In ruku', you glorify your Lord."

The beautiful part of salah is when you engaged in ruku', you bow down – put your head down before Allah s.w.t. There is a spiritual state your heart cannot access unless your body is actually in that position. That is the beautiful connection between body and mind, between your physical existence and the spiritual part of who you are.

The Prophet s.a.w says, "In ruku', you glorify your Lord." That is a clear expression. You are expressing the fact that you feel the glory of Allah s.w.t and you appreciate not only with words, but even with your physical stance. You are expressing your recognition of Allah's greatness and that you love it. You are showing that you want to live by those beautiful meanings.

Therefore, ruku' is such a beautiful expression of your humility before Allah s.w.t. When you go through that randomly, it does not have an impact on you. However, when you are aware of this beautiful meanings, it takes you to a completely different world.

#24 Stand in Thankfulness

Thank Allah s.w.t for the privilege of ruku'

After you are done with your ruku', you go back to standing up. There is a question that probably comes to your mind: Why don't I just go to sujood?

There is a point for you to take a step back and stand up straight. That is basically to take in that miraculous moment of khushu'. It is to allow yourself to reflect on it. This moment is also for you to express your thanks and your gratitude to Allah s.w.t for offering you such a privilege, where He allowed you to bow in front of Him and experience that beautiful state. Therefore, you are taking a moment back and you are standing up, then you say (which means), "Allah hears from the one who praises Him; all praises due to Allah."

Basically you take that moment to praise Allah s.w.t for allowing you the privilege of bowing before Him. You will feel really taking care of through the gift that Allah s.w.t made obligatory upon us, which is the salah.

#25 The Secrets of Sujood

Sujood is the heart of the prayer

After you have make ruku' and you have stood up again, it is time to go to the most unique experience in salah. It is really the heart of salah.

Basically when you put your forehead on the ground for your Creator, you recognize your humility and His greatness. You are not expressing that only with your words and your tongue, you are expressing that with your entirety. Therefore, your body, tongue, and heart are all engaged in it.

Before you go down for sujood, make sure you are actually ready for that most important moment in your salah.

#26 Profound Servitude

Sujood is the time to get the closest to Allah

We are now talking about the beautiful state of sujood. There is a surprise for you. The Prophet s.a.w says, "The closest that a person could get to Allah is when they are in the state of sujood (prostration)." [Sahih, recorded by Imam Muslim]

When you prostrate and you put your body down because you recognize Allah s.w.t is The Most High, that is the most profound statement and expression of servitude. That is why Allah s.w.t rewards you by being the closest to Him when you are actually there. It sounds like contradiction. But this defies what we know about physical reality.

Therefore, sujood is the time to get the closest to Allah s.w.t. Your heart and mind need to be there fully. Do not engage in anything else in the world and do not miss out in this beautiful meaning because it is part of Paradise. Then you will find your khushu'.

#27 The Closest to Allah

Open up to Allah s.w.t when you are in sujood

You are already in the state of khushu' – you put your forehead, your hands, and knees on the floor; your body is down while recognizing the highness and the greatness of Allah s.w.t. Then it is time for word. It is time to ask Allah s.w.t because you are at the closest position to Him. Now it is the time to feel your helplessness in comparison to Allah's might and power.

It is the time when you open up to Allah s.w.t and you leave the whole world behind. You turn to Allah s.w.t expressing yourself fully to Him. Therefore, do not just put your forehead on the ground and get back again. Do not do that. Do not rush through sujood. Allow yourself to settle in there – your body and heart will settle and then your soul will enjoy it.

You are the closest to Allah s.w.t. This is an experience out of this world. Therefore, call upon Allah s.w.t. Whatever you want from Him, ask and tell Him to grant that to you. You will see how your connection to Allah s.w.t will be unforgettable.

#28 A Prayer of Peace

Seal your prayer in the best way that Allah s.w.t would be pleased with

You have performed your sujood, you stood up again or you sat back again, then you went back to another sujood which actually serves as an act of gratitude – thanking Allah s.w.t for the first sujood. This is because you can never get enough of sujood if you truly engage in it.

After that, you have to conclude your salah. You do this by just connecting to Allah s.w.t – you make your tasyahhud and salawat Ibrahimiyah. Then ultimately you conclude your salah with "Assalamualaikum warahmatullah". Sealing your prayer with peace. Realizing that salah really brings you peace to your heart. Why? Because it makes you the best you can, it brings out the best potential in you.

Salah is an act of being a full human beings, tapping into the best in who you are and what you are. Therefore, when you are concluding your salah, do not just go through it. Make sure you seal it with the best impression and feeling. Seal it in the best way that Allah s.w.t would be pleased with.

Reflect on the blessings of being engaged in salah and being offered this beautiful gift of Allah s.w.t repeatedly and you will see your khushu' will rise up again.

Conclusion and The Big Secret of Khushu'

Khushu' is a gift from Allah s.w.t.

It is the fact that khushu' is not in your hand. Khushu' is a gift from Allah s.w.t. If you really want to get it, you need to ask Allah s.w.t. and you need to do that with so much sincerity and dedication.

What I share with you in this book are tactics and tips to help you get more khushu' and qualified for high level of khushu'. If you really have gone through the whole thing and you put your heart in it, Allah s.w.t will not let you down. The best way to get khushu' is to open up and let Allah s.w.t give it to you.

Oftentimes, we try to manufacture our khushu', we force it, or try to do it by sheer willpower, but the more you do it this way, the more it escapes you. Khushu' is a gift from Allah s.w.t. Therefore you need to be ready for it, you need to open up, and you need to let Him bring it to your heart. It is important to be in a state of surrendering and accepting to achieve khushu' in our prayer.

9 789671 740224